Xtermigator's Big Heart, Learning about Unseen Disabilities

XTERMIGATOR
-& THE -
ZOOMY FROG

DR. ERIC FISHON & DR. JENNIFER MARAZZO

XTERMIGATOR AND THE ZOOMY FROG

XTERMIGATOR'S BIG HEART, Learning about Unseen Disabilities

Friendly Ferns Publishing 2025

XTERMIGATOR KIDS ™

Smithtown, NY

eric@xtermigatorkids.com - jennifer@xtermigatorkids.com

www.xtermigatorkids.com - A Dr. Disruptor Initiative

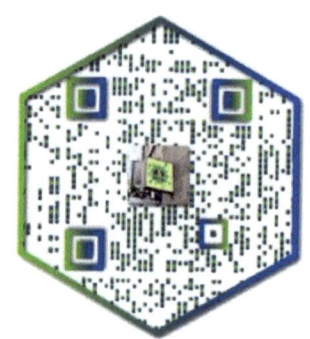

LCCN 2025903689

Paperback ISBN 9781967331024

Hardcover ISBN 9781967331017

Digital ISBN 9781967331048

AT THE HEART OF THIS BEAUTIFUL PLACE STANDS A GATOR NAMED XTERMIGATOR, AN ALLIGATOR WITH A BIG HEART AND AN EVEN BIGGER MAGNIFYING GLASS. HE IS ALWAYS READY TO HELP HIS FRIENDS WITH KINDNESS AND A CURIOUS MIND. GET TO KNOW THE XTERMIGATOR AND ALL OF HIS FRIENDS IN THIS BEAUTIFULLY CRAFTED SERIES DEDICATED TO BREAKING BARRIERS FOR CHILDREN WITH UNSEEN DISABILITIES AND PROMOTING THE MOTTO: "A DISABILITY IS NOT AN INABILITY."

THROUGH HEARTWARMING STORIES AND VIBRANT ILLUSTRATIONS, THIS SERIES FOSTERS INCLUSIVITY, UNDERSTANDING AND EMPOWERMENT FOR CHILDREN WHO MAY EXPERIENCE CHALLENGES THAT AREN'T ALWAYS VISIBLE.

EACH BOOK INTRODUCES READERS TO DIVERSE CHARACTERS WHO NAVIGATE THE WORLD IN THEIR OWN UNIQUE WAYS, ENCOURAGING KINDNESS, EMPATHY, AND AWARENESS. WHETHER IT IS ADHD, SENSORY SENSITIVITIES OR OTHER HIDDEN STRUGGLES, THE XTERMIGATOR AND HIS FRIENDS SHOW THAT EVERY CHILD HAS INCREDIBLE STRENGTHS AND DESERVES TO BE SEEN, UNDERSTOOD, AND CELEBRATED.

JOIN THE ADVENTURE AND DISCOVER A WORLD WHERE DIFFERENCES ARE EMBRACED AND EVERY CHILD SHINES!

In the Friendly Ferns Swamp, there lived a happy little frog named Freddy. Freddy loved to jump, splash, and explore!

But sometimes, Freddy's Zoomies made things a little tricky.

"Why can't I catch even one little fly today?! My legs won't stop hopping around!" Freddy's frustration grew as his jittery legs kept him bouncing in all directions.

What are the Zoomies, you ask?

Well, they're like fireworks in your brain— bright, fast, and full of energy!

Some days, Freddy's Zoomies made him bounce from one idea to the next.

Other days, they made it hard to sit still and listen.

One sunny morning, Daisy the Dragonfly was telling Freddy a story about her latest flying adventure.

"...And then I swooped right over the tallest cattail!", Daisy said excitedly.

Freddy tried to listen, he really did! But... BZZZ! A bee zipped by.

SPLASH! A fish jumped in the water.

RUSTLE! The wind made the lily pads dance.

Freddy's mind jumped from one thing to the next.

"Freddy, are you even listening?" Daisy huffed, crossing her tiny arms.

Freddy's eyes widened. "Oh! Uh… something about cattails?"

Daisy sighed. "You have the Zoomies again, don't you?"

Freddy nodded. "I can't help it! My brain just goes, GO, GO, GO!"

Just then, XTERMIGATOR stepped forward from a thicket of tall grass.

"Hmm," he said, stroking his chin. "It sounds like your brain is super-fast and super creative! But it also makes it hard to focus, right?"

Freddy nodded.

"I've seen this before," XTERMIGATOR said with a wink. "Your Zoomies remind me of something called ADHD."

"AD... what now?" Freddy asked, tilting his head.

"ADHD!" XTERMIGATOR explained. "It means your brain is like a race car—really fast and full of ideas. But sometimes, it needs help steering."

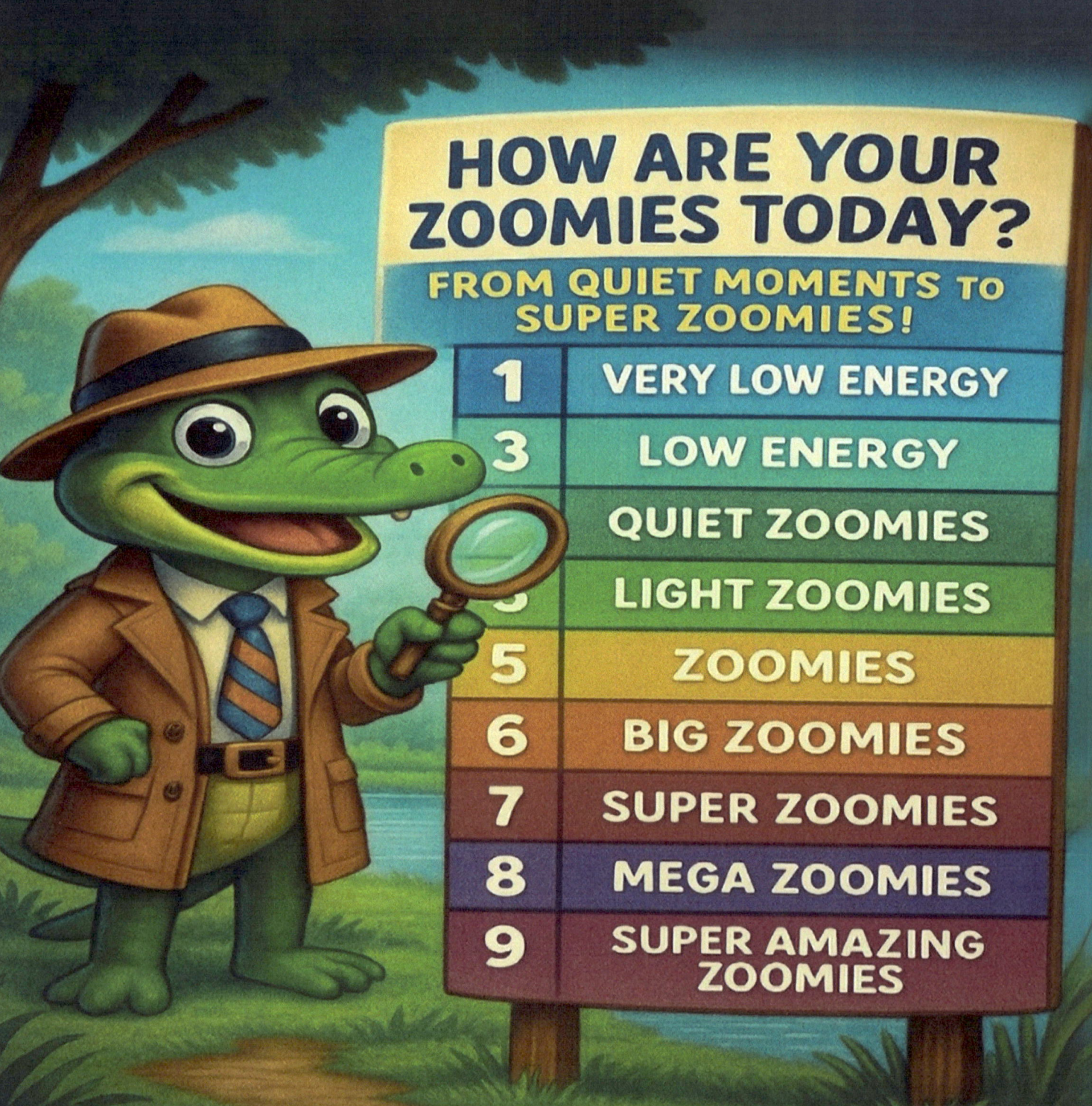

"There are different kinds of Zoomies," XTERMIGATOR said.

"Super Zoomies – When your energy is extra high, your legs bounce, your brain races, and you just have to move!"

"Then there are Quiet Zoomies – Sometimes, you may just stare into space. Your brain is still moving fast, but it's like a daydream dance."

Super Zoomies or Quiet Zoomies—no matter the type, they're part of what makes you unique!"

"How can I ever catch anything when I'm this zoomy?!" Freddy asked as he zipped from one lily pad to another, making flies buzz away in all directions.

"You can do it!" XTERMIGATOR explained. "Zoomies aren't bad; they just need a little help!"

Freddy leaned in. "Like what?"

"Try one thing at a time. If you're talking to a friend, look at their eyes. If you need to move, wiggle your toes or bounce softly." If you need to take a sbreak, take some deep breaths or draw a picture.

Freddy tried it. He wiggled his toes, took a deep breath, and bounced from lily pad to lily pad, taking his time.

"I can do this", Freddy said. The XTERMIGATOR watched proudly as Freddy focused on the nearby flies.

"Thanks, XTERMIGATOR!, said Freddie. Talking to you and taking one thing at a time really helps. I feel like a super special frog already!"

"Taking brain breaks are just fine too." Said XTERMIGATOR. "Find a comfy lily pad to relax and allow your body to unwind." Having a calm and cozy spot can help you feel more in control and let your brain stay focused.

Freddy took a deep breath. "So, having Zoomies doesn't mean something is wrong with me?"

XTERMIGATOR shook his head. "Nope! It just means your brain is awesome in its own way."

Freddy smiled. "Then I guess my Zoomies make me... ME!"

Freddy's friends wanted to help too!

Shelly the Turtle said, "We can take breaks during games so you don't feel rushed." Romeeo the Cat added, "We can make a checklist to help you stay on track!"

Daisy the Dragonfly grinned. "And I'll remind you when I need your full attention!"

Freddy smiled as he looked around at his friends and the peaceful swamp. He had learned that his Zoomies weren't something to hide—they were part of what made him special. With new tricks and the support of his friends, he felt ready for any adventure that lay ahead.

Freddy's Toolbox: Strategies for Managing ADHD

Congratulations on finishing Freddie's adventure! Here's a special toolbox with all the helpful strategies that Freddie learned along the way. These tips are designed to support children and their families in understanding and managing ADHD in a fun and empowering way.

1. Take Brain Breaks

What Freddie Learned: Short breaks can help reset your focus and give you energy.

Try This:

- Set a timer for work and play. 15 minutes of focus followed by 5 minutes of movement.

- Do frog hops, stretches, or a quick dance to refresh your mind.

Why It Works: Movement helps release energy and improve concentration.

"Taking breaks doesn't slow you down—it helps your brain recharge like a battery!"

2. Create a 'Quiet Lily Pad' Space

What Freddie Learned: A calm, cozy spot can help when distractions feel overwhelming.

Try This:

• Find a quiet corner for reading, homework, or just relaxing. • Use headphones or soft music to block background noise.

Why It Works: Reducing sensory input helps kids stay focused and calm.

3. Hop by Hop, Not All at Once

What Freddie Learned: Taking things one step at a time is okay. **Try This:**

• Make a list of tasks and check them off one by one. • Break big tasks into smaller, manageable steps.

Why It Works: Small accomplishments build confidence and prevent overwhelm. "Remember: Small hops lead to big adventures! Celebrate each little win."

4. Celebrate Small Wins

What Freddie Learned: Every small victory deserves a celebration. **Try This:**

• Reward yourself with a high-five or a "job well done" after completing a task. • Keep a success journal to track daily wins.

Why It Works: Positive reinforcement helps build motivation and self-esteem.

5. Catch the Thought

What Freddie Learned: Practicing mindfulness helps with focus. **Try This:**

• Take deep breaths when feeling overwhelmed.

• Imagine capturing a buzzing thought, akin to a fly, and gently releasing it.

Why It Works: Mindfulness helps calm the brain and refocus attention.

6.   Stay Organized with Visual Tools

What Freddie Learned: Visual reminders help stay on track. **Try This:**

• Use colorful sticky notes, charts, or reminder alarms. • Create a daily or weekly schedule with fun stickers.

Why It Works: Visual aids make tasks easier to remember and complete.

7.   Use Energy Wisely

What Freddie Learned: Being active is essential, as is knowing when to rest. **Try This:**

• Balance high-energy activities with calming ones like reading or drawing.
• Try short relaxation exercises like deep breathing or quiet reflection.

Why It Works: Managing energy helps prevent burnout and keeps the brain alert.

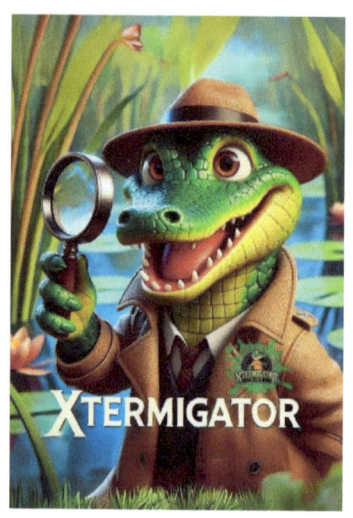

XTERMIGATOR

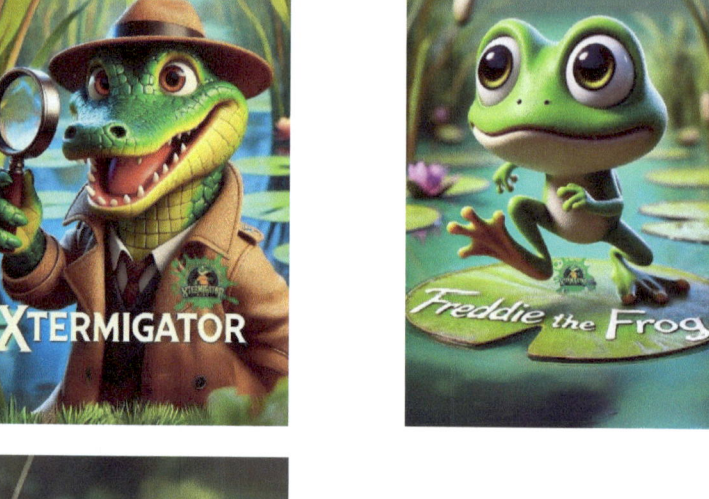

Freddie the Frog

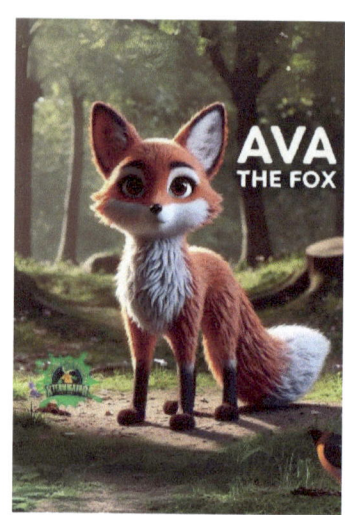

AVA THE FOX

Oliver
THE OTTER

FRIENDLY FERNS
PUBLISHING

DR. DISRUPTOR

Romeeo
THE CAT

Shelly
THE TURTLE

Tebow the Cat

MEET THE

FRIENDLY FERNS
SWAMP

FRIENDS

XTERMIGATOR

Well, howdy there, friend!

The name's Xtermigator, but you can just call me X! I'm the friendly detective of these here swampy parts, always on the lookout for a good mystery—especially the kind you can't see with your eyes alone.

You see, not all challenges are as clear as a muddy footprint or a missing lily pad. Some of the trickiest ones are hidden deep inside, where only patience, understanding, and a little detective work can uncover the truth.

In our adventures, we'll uncover the hidden strengths inside each of us

—because everyone's got 'em! With a little curiosity, creativity, and kindness, we'll crack the case and find ways to make life in the swamp just right for everyone. So, what do you say?

Ready to join me on a new adventure? Let's get sleuthing!

Hey there, HOPPY to meet you!

I'm Freddie the Frog, the fastest, jumpiest, most excitable critter in the whole swamp! I've got Zoomies—that's what I call it when my brain is bouncing with ideas, my feet just won't stay still, and I feel like I need to leap in ten different directions all at once!

Now, don't get me wrong—I love being full of energy! It makes me great at thinking up wild ideas, playing new games, and keeping my friends laughing. But sometimes, my Zoomies make things a little tricky. Like when I try to listen but get distracted by a buzzing dragonfly... or when I start a project but never quite finish because—oh wow, did you see that butterfly?!

I'm learning that my energy isn't a problem—it's my superpower! I just have to find ways to use it right. So, if you've ever felt like your mind is zooming around faster than a firefly at sundown, you're not alone! Stick with me, and we'll figure it out together. Now, who's ready for an adventure?

Let's JUMP in!

Oliver
THE OTTER

Oh... hi there. Um... is it okay if I introduce myself?

I'm Ollie the Otter, and, well... I get nervous a lot. Some things—like big crowds, loud noises, or trying something new—make my tummy feel all twisty. But the thing that scares me the most? Water. I know, I know... an otter afraid of water? It sounds silly. But when I get too close, my paws start shaking, my heart races, and I just can't make myself jump in. I wish I could be brave like my friends, but sometimes, my worries feel bigger than me. What if I can't do it? What if I make a mistake? What if everyone laughs?

I'm learning to take deep breaths, imagine happy places, and remind myself that it's okay to be scared—but fear doesn't have to stop me. And you know what? Every time I face my fears, even just a little bit, I feel stronger. Maybe, just maybe, one day I'll find the courage to swim. If you ever feel nervous like me, don't worry—you're not alone. We can be brave together, one small step at a time.

Tebow the Cat

Pssst... over here! No, over here!

Whoosh!

Oh, wait—you found me! Hey there, I'm Tebow the Cat—swift as a shadow, sneaky as a whisper, and always ready for an adventure! You never know where I'll pop up next... maybe behind a tree, under a hat, or right in the middle of a super serious moment—oops! But don't worry, I'm here to help... in my own special way.

See, life can get pretty tricky for my friends. Sometimes, worries get big, or focus gets fuzzy, and that's when I swoop in with a purr-fectly timed joke or a game of chase to lighten the mood. Because no matter how tough things feel, a little laughter, a little fun, and maybe a tiny bit of mischief can make the swamp feel brighter. But don't let my playful paws fool you—I always have my friends' backs. Whether it's a tough day or a tough challenge, I'm there to remind them that joy is just around the corner... sometimes you just have to pounce on it!

So, what do you say? Ready to stir up some fun? Let's go!

But, uh... if Xtermigator asks, you didn't see me knock over that stack of books, okay?

Shelly
THE TURTLE

Oh, hello there. I'm so glad you stopped by! My name is Shelly the Turtle, and I like to take things slow and steady—not just because I'm a turtle, but because my body needs lots of rest. You see, I get tired a lot, even when I haven't done much at all. Some days, my legs feel heavy, my head feels foggy, and even simple things—like keeping up with my friends—can feel really hard.

At first, I didn't understand why I couldn't move as fast or do as much as everyone else. I worried that if I rested too much, I'd be left behind. But then I learned something important: rest isn't a weakness—it's what makes me stronger.

With the help of Xtermigator and my wonderful friends, I'm learning to listen to my body, take breaks when I need to, and never feel bad for going at my own pace. And you know what?

Slowing down helps me notice the little things—the way the sunlight sparkles on the water, the gentle rustle of the trees, the kindness in a friend's smile. So, if you ever feel like the world is moving too fast, that's okay. You can sit with me for a while. We'll take a deep breath, rest, and remember that our own pace is the perfect pace. Want to take a slow and steady adventure with me?

A disability is not an inability

XTERMIGATOR
KIDS

ROMEEO
THE CAT

Hello, friend. You can sit with me for a while if you'd like.

I'm Romeo, a brown-and-gold cat with a soft purr and a big heart. I may not be the fastest like Freddie, the sneakiest like Tebow, or the bravest like Xtermigator, but I have a special gift—I listen.

Sometimes, my friends feel anxious, frustrated, or just plain tired, and that's when I do what I do best. I curl up beside them, offer a gentle nudge, or simply sit close, letting them know they're never alone. I may not have all the answers, but I know that a little kindness, a quiet moment, or a warm presence can make even the heaviest days feel lighter.

I see things others might not notice—the way Ollie's whiskers twitch when he's nervous, the way Shelly's shoulders droop when she's too tired, or the way Freddy's paws tap when his thoughts are racing. And when I do, I remind them: You are seen. You are understood. You are enough.If you ever need a friend to sit with you in the quiet, I'll be here. No rush, no pressure—just a steady heart and a soft purr, reminding you that you are never alone.Would you like to take a deep breath with me?

AVA
THE FOX

Hello. I'm Ava. I like routines. I like knowing what comes next. I like when things make sense.

I don't like surprises. Or loud noises. Or when plans change at the last minute. When that happens, my brain feels like a tangled-up ball of yarn, and I don't know how to fix it. Sometimes, my big feelings take over before I even understand them.

But there are things that help. Like deep breaths. Or counting in my head. Or finding a quiet place to reset. And I have wonderful friends— like Xtermigator, Shelly, and Romeo—who remind me that even when things don't go as planned, I am safe.

I may not always understand the way others think, and they may not always understand me. But that's okay. Because my way of seeing the world is special— I notice details that others miss, I can focus on tricky problems, and I am very, very good at things I love.

Change is hard, but I'm learning that sometimes, it can bring good things too. And even when the world feels too much, I know I am never alone.

Would you like to go on an adventure with me? Don't worry—I'll make us a plan!

Positive Affirmations

ADHD is something that makes people's brains work a little differently.

Being different is OKAY!

Feeling frustrated is OKAY! Let's hop into a plan together.

Teamwork makes every hop easier!

With friends like yours, you'll always find a way forward.

Positive Affirmations

Your Zoomies make you unique!

When you learn to guide them, there's no stopping what you can do!

Just like Freddy, you have your own unique strengths. No challenge is too big when you take it hop by hop, with courage and kindness in your heart.

Now, let's take a look at some helpful tips that you can try too!

A Note to Parents and Caregivers

ADHD is a unique way of experiencing the world. By celebrating your child's strengths and supporting them with practical tools, you can help them thrive. Remember, every child is different, so finding what works best may take time and patience. Just like Freddie learned, small steps lead to big success!

Find educational and entertaining resources for children at www.xtermigatorkids.com

Different is beautiful. Together, we are unstoppable!

"The resources listed here are for informational purposes only and do not constitute professional medical advice. Please consult with your child's healthcare providers for personalized guidance."

As you close this book and reflect on its message, consider this cover a symbol of hidden stories. For those living with unseen disabilities, their journey is often a kaleidoscope of colors and experiences others may not notice, But within this complexity lies resilience, strength, and purpose. Just like this cover, unseen layers create something meaningful when you take the time to look closer. May this book inspire you to look beyond the obvious and embrace the beauty of the hidden.

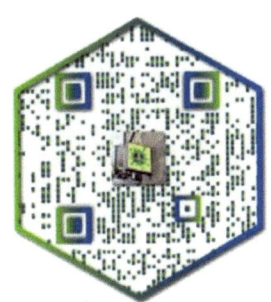

About the Authors

Dr. Eric Fishon (Dr. Disruptor) is an author, advocate, and educator dedicated to championing inclusivity, particularly for individuals with unseen disabilities. Through his books, research, and platform, Dr. Disruptor, he challenges societal norms and empowers people to embrace their unique strengths. His work spans memoirs, academic research, and children's literature, including the XTERMIGATOR KIDS series, which fosters understanding and self-acceptance among young readers.

Dr. Fishon's background includes extensive research on disability advocacy, emotional intelligence, and stress regulation, particularly for individuals with autoimmune conditions. He is actively involved in higher education, with a focus on inclusive policies and the intersection of mental health, accessibility, and academic success. His writing seamlessly blends personal experience with academic insights, offering practical guidance for individuals navigating education, workplaces, and faith communities with unseen disabilities.

Through his podcast, Plugged Into Your Day, and interactive online initiatives, Dr. Fishon continues to disrupt outdated perspectives, creating a world where difference is celebrated and accessibility is the norm.

His motto, "A Disability is not an Inability, it's your greatest Superpower!", reflects his unwavering commitment to fostering a more inclusive and understanding society.

For more about his work, visit drdisruptors.com.

About the Authors

Dr. Jennifer Marazzo, DHA, CBIS, CHFP, FACHDM, is a passionate advocate, accomplished healthcare leader, and inspirational author committed to transforming adversity into impact. As a fierce champion for individuals with unseen disabilities, she empowers others to turn limitations into legacies.

With a distinguished career in healthcare administration, financial management, and brain injury specialization, Dr. Marazzo believes that challenges are not barriers but stepping stones to greatness. She has dedicated her life to advocating for those whose voices often go unheard, ensuring that every person—regardless of circumstance—is seen, heard, and valued.

Through her writing, Dr. Marazzo weaves together stories of resilience, hope, and transformation. As the Founder and Co-Creator of XTERMIGATOR KIDS, LLC, and Dr. Disruptor, LLC, she is committed to helping children and adults alike embrace their unique strengths and redefine their futures. Whether through leadership, mentorship, research or storytelling, her mission remains unwavering: to illuminate paths where others see obstacles and to inspire people to forge legacies that transcend any boundaries.

Her motto, "Different is beautiful, together we are unstoppable" stands as a commitment to advancing innovative practices in the evolution of inclusivity for people with unseen disabilities.

Jennifer Marazzo

Acknowledgements

This story is the heart of a movement—to bring the unseen to light, to give a voice to the voiceless. There are countless stories of struggle and overcoming, and this book is just one thread in a much larger tapestry of resilience, hope, and courage.

To those like us who have walked difficult paths, who have fought to be heard, and who continue to rise despite the odds—this book is for you. Your strength inspires, your stories matter, and your voices deserve to be amplified.

A heartfelt thank you to all of our family, friends, and mentors who have supported this journey, offering wisdom, encouragement, and unwavering belief.

To Tyler Stavros - for inspiring all that I do, and creating these characters with me as well as bringing out the best in me. To Tara - Thank you for opening up your heart, family, and world for me to become Tyler's Ba Ba.

To Ava- for your joy, love, and inspiration. You are the light of my life and the best part of me.

To our readers—thank you for opening your hearts to this story. May it inspire you to listen, to see, and to uplift those whose voices have long been unheard.

Together, we can shine a light in the darkest places.

This cover is more than an illustration—it's a window into a world often misunderstood. For those of us with unseen disabilities, life can feel like this image: vibrant, layered, and full of mystery that isn't always visible on the surface.

What others see is often just on the surface—colorful and calm—but beneath that lies a unique depth of challenges, strength, and determination. This book is an invitation to step into that world, to see what is not seen on the surface but the beauty that lies within...

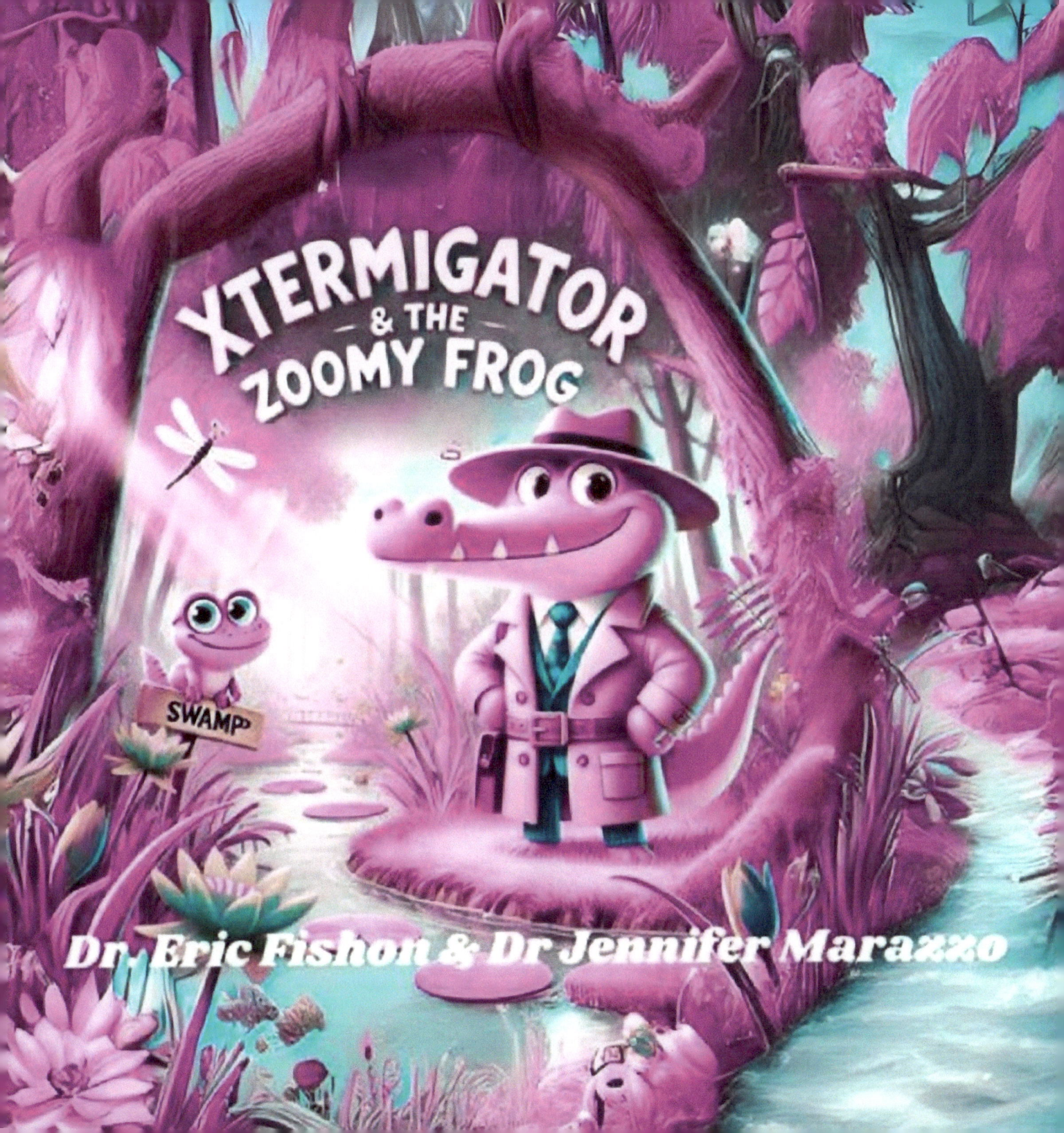